EVERYDAY PRODUCTIVITY

Peter Mulraney

Copyright © 2017 Peter Mulraney

All rights reserved.

No part of this book may be reproduced in any form or by any electronic or mechanical means, including information storage and retrieval systems, without written permission from the author, except for the use of brief quotations in a book review.

ISBN-13: 978-0-6482523-5-1

This edition published 2018.

CONTENTS

Introduction	1
How To Use This Book	2
Overview	3
3 Secret Ingredients Of Productivity	6
Lifestyle	9
Lifestyle Self-Audit	12
Lifestyle Action Plan	23
Attitude	29
Attitude Self-Audit	32
Attitude Action Plan	36
Work environment	40
Work Environment Self-Audit	43
Work Environment Action Plan	47
Habits	50
Habits Self-Audit	51
Habits Action Plan	59
Tools	64
Tools Self-Audit	65
Tools Action Plan	69
Skills	72
Skills Self-Audit	73
Skills Action Plan	82
Knowledge	86
Knowledge Self-Audit	88
Knowledge Action Plan	92

Community	94
Community Self-Audit	95
Community Action Plan	97
Summary	99
Further reading	100
A Note From Peter	101
Also by Peter Mulraney	102

INTRODUCTION

If you're interested in productivity, you're no doubt looking for ways to work smarter so that you'll get more done. In fact, you're probably looking for apps to help you get things done faster and with less effort. After all, you live in a digital world that promises streamlining and efficiency.

Surprisingly, or not so surprisingly for those of us who have been around for a while, there are steps you can take to work smarter that don't involve apps at all. Some of the most effective ways of increasing your productivity are simple things like getting more sleep, drinking less booze, changing your diet and doing some exercise. They don't cost much but they do require something that all productive people know about: self-discipline.

Self-discipline allows you to move from dreaming through planning to action and to persevere until you reach your goal. It's a choice to act. It's not restricted to champions. You choose to be self-disciplined – it doesn't happen any other way.

I have nothing against productivity apps and use several myself but this is not a book about apps. This is a book about developing a productive mindset that you can apply to all areas of your life, not just during the hours you spend at work. In addition to self-discipline, a productive mindset requires self-awareness, that is, being aware of how your own behaviours and attitudes impact on your performance and the performance of others.

The strategy for developing a productive mindset offered in these pages involves an examination of eight areas that influence productivity, an analysis of your current position, and the construction of action plans to help you refocus your efforts and be more productive.

If you're not interested in applying a little self-honesty to an examination of your current behaviours and attitudes or in making a commitment to yourself to become more productive, put this book back on the shelf - there are no magic tricks inside.

On the other hand, if you are ready to develop a more productive mindset and to apply it to everything you do, then turn the page and join me for a journey through your attitudes and behaviours that will set you on a path to doing more with your life.

How To Use This Book

The structure of this book provides a focus on each of eight areas that influence productivity:

- Lifestyle
- Attitude
- Work Environment
- Habits
- Tools
- Skills
- Knowledge
- Community

In each focus area, you'll be guided through a self-analysis exercise and then asked to construct an action plan based on the findings of your self-analysis.

The end result of completing the exercises will be a reframing of your understanding of how your behaviours and attitudes impact on your productivity. It's that reframing which will help you develop a more productive mindset.

I suggest you read through the book before starting on the self-analysis exercises, and then come back and work on the areas that appeal to you the most. This is not something you should expect to complete over a weekend. This work takes time and will be ongoing.

The focus area you choose to start with is up to you, but I recommend you consider starting with lifestyle.

This book is designed as a workbook. In each section, you will find space to complete the self-audits and compile the action plans - but don't let that space limit your responses. Feel free to work outside the book in a journal or on a computer. The essential step is completing the exercises.

Overview

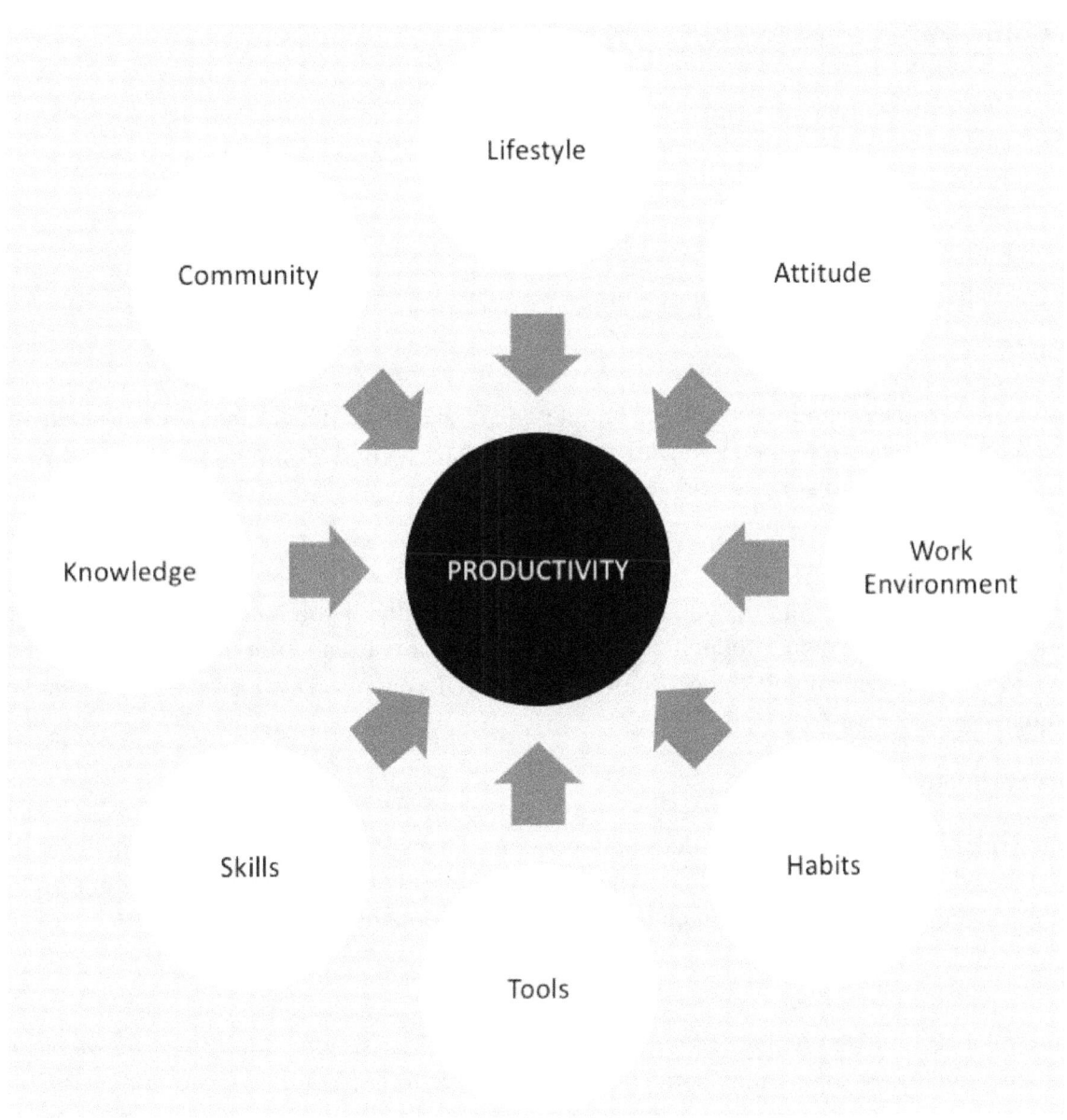

Productivity

Productivity in the workplace is a measure of your effectiveness - with a focus on both the quality and quantity of the work you do.

Your personal productivity is influenced by a range of factors:

- Lifestyle
- Attitude
- Work Environment
- Habits
- Tools
- Skills
- Knowledge
- Community

Lifestyle

Lifestyle is about how you live your life. Your lifestyle choices may be affecting your productivity in the workplace. The secret is becoming aware of how what you're doing when you're not at work is influencing your performance at work.

Attitude

Attitude or mindset is about how you approach things mentally. If you hate your job, you're going to find it difficult to be more productive. If you're set in your ways and not open to change, you're going to struggle with doing things differently, which is often a key ingredient for increasing productivity.

Work Environment

If you work in an environment that does not encourage change or innovation, you're likely to meet resistance whenever you try something different. Sometimes you have to take a risk and lead from where you are, even if you aren't in charge. And, more importantly, when you are.

Habits

Your daily habits either facilitate or impede your productivity. You need to bring your habits into awareness and assess their value. Some of them may have to go. You may need to develop some new ones.

Tools

Tools are the things you use to help you do your job. Your level of mastery of the tools available to you and the nature of those tools affect your productivity.

Skills

Every job requires a particular set of skills. Not having the proper skills or not keeping up with changes as your job evolves hinders your productivity. Skills are like tools in that your level of mastery influences your productivity, and mastery requires an ongoing commitment to your own education.

Knowledge

What you know about your job or your role in the workplace, and, just as importantly, what you don't know about it affect your productivity. You have some level of workplace knowledge but unless you bring it into awareness you can't use it constructively.

Community

We are all surrounded by people, and the people around you influence your productivity to the extent that they support you or not. In some cases, your measured productivity depends upon the actions of others, where your challenge is to lead them to the level of performance you want to achieve.

If you want to increase your productivity, you need to address each of these factors.

3 Secret Ingredients Of Productivity

Before we examine the factors that influence your productivity in detail, let's take a moment to think about what it means to be productive in the workplace.

Being productive is more than just being busy. You've no doubt had days when you were busy all day but, at the end of the day, felt as if you hadn't actually achieved anything. I know I have.

Work is something we do with intent. It has a purpose. It's not just a way of passing the time. You generally don't get paid for that.

Being productive at work or in your own business is about getting things done that you want to get done for a specific reason, and I don't mean so you'll get paid. That's a by-product of being productive.

Contrary to what many people think, business is about service. It's about producing goods and providing services that others need or want. If you're being productive, then what you are doing is contributing to either the production or delivery of those goods and services. When you're not being productive, then, basically, you're not contributing.

If you're reading this, it's probably safe to assume that you're interested in contributing by being productive in your chosen field and that you want to be as productive as possible. After all, we live in a society that rewards people for being productive, and there's nothing wrong with being paid for making a contribution.

As I mentioned in the overview, there are a lot of factors that can either help or hinder your efforts to be productive. There are three other things, though, what we might call the **three secret ingredients**, that are more important than all of those factors: awareness, purpose, and action.

Awareness

You can't do anything about things of which you are not aware. You can probably recall a time when someone at school stuck a sign on another student's back as an April Fool's joke. It was a laugh for everyone - except for the poor person totally unaware of the sign. You don't want to be that person in the workplace.

The focus of this book is on helping you bring things into awareness so you can (1) assess their impact on your productivity, and (2) do something about them.

Purpose

It's important to be aware of the purpose of your work, as it's less likely that you'll be productive when you don't know what you're working to achieve.

Take some time to identify the purpose of your work. This might take a moment or it may require a little research. You may need to review your vision statement or think about articulating one for your business, or you may need to read your duty statement or job description.

I'll come back to purpose in the chapters on attitude and knowledge but I suggest you stop and answer the appropriate question below before reading the next chapter.

- If you're an employee - what is it that you're being paid to do each day?
- If you're self-employed - why do you get up and go to work every day?

Action

There is no point in knowing all there is to know about being productive if you don't take action, and not just any action. If you want to be productive you need to take action aligned with your purpose.

THE PURPOSE OF MY WORK IS:

LIFESTYLE

By lifestyle, I mean how you're living your life, so my focus is on what you do when you're not at work. One of the reasons I chose to start with lifestyle is that it's something you can address without drawing attention to yourself at work. It's also an easy way to show you that you can do something about your behaviours - once you become aware of them and their potential consequences beyond your front door.

Sleep deprivation

If you're still wondering what influence your lifestyle choices could possibly have on your productivity, type 'sleep deprivation' into your search engine of choice and hit 'enter'.

Here's a list, compiled by Better Health Victoria, of some of the effects of sleep deprivation that relate directly to work performance.

- Reduced alertness
- Shortened attention span
- Slower than normal reaction time
- Poor judgement
- Reduced awareness of the environment and situation
- Reduced decision-making skills
- Poor memory
- Reduced concentration
- Increased likelihood of mentally 'stalling' or fixating on one thought
- Increased likelihood of moodiness and bad temper
- Reduced work efficiency
- Loss of motivation
- Errors of omission – making a mistake by forgetting to do something
- Errors of commission – making a mistake by doing something, but choosing the wrong option
- Micro-sleep – brief periods of involuntary sleeping that range from a few seconds to a few minutes in duration.

Living in separate boxes

We tend to divide our work and home lives into separate boxes and ignore the impacts each has on the other. You're no doubt familiar with stories about workaholics, people who destroy their family lives by spending too much time at work. Those stories actually illustrate the interconnectedness of the different parts of your life, so it's really not all that surprising, when you think about it, that your home life can affect your work life, and, therefore, your productivity. And, it's not just your sleeping pattern. It's all those things that generate stress in your life.

Relationships

If things are going well in your relationship with your significant other, chances are you're feeling good about going to work and the state of your relationship is not distracting you from the task at hand. If, on the other hand, you're experiencing some relationship issues, you're probably finding it difficult to concentrate on the job. You may even be having some trouble sleeping, and we've already seen what that can do. This is one aspect of your life you can do something about if it's causing you stress and affecting your productivity. You might only need to talk to your partner. You might need to make some behavioural changes or get help to sort out your issues. You may need to end the relationship. Point is, you can either do something about it or simply hope it will go away. The choice is yours.

Money

Most money problems are self-inflicted. Sure, there will be times when something comes out of left field that you weren't expecting but, if you're honest with yourself, you'll know that your money problems are the result of spending more than you earn. Take a look at your credit cards. They exist to allow you to do just that.

If you're worrying about how you're going to pay this month's bills when you're supposed to be working, you will not be as productive as you could be. The good news is money problems are fixable, if you're prepared to exercise some self-control when it comes to spending. But, again, the choice is yours to make.

Health and fitness

Sometimes you can be your own worst enemy, especially when it comes to how you look after your body. You eat fast food. You settle for being a couch potato. You mess with your brain chemistry by drinking too much alcohol or using so-called recreational drugs and narcotics or overusing medical opiates. You reduce your lung capacity by smoking cigarettes or weed, despite all the health warnings on the packet. If you're a 'party animal', you might want to go back and read that list of effects of sleep deprivation and ask yourself why they do blood tests and impose sleep restrictions on pilots and people operating machinery in underground mines. You might only be operating a computer but you'll face the same problems.

When you think about it, you don't need to be a rocket scientist to work out that if you're overweight, unfit, and mess with your brain chemistry and lung capacity, you probably won't be at your best when you turn up for work.

But there's more to wellbeing than physical fitness and healthy eating habits. There's also how you look after yourself from a mental or spiritual perspective. If you want to operate optimally in the workplace, you need to give yourself some downtime and have some fun. You're not going to be productive if you're running on empty most of the time. Fortunately, there are ways of addressing these issues but they all require one thing: self-discipline.

Family responsibilities

The extent of your family responsibilities changes with time. If you have young children, they get sick, they have trouble sleeping, and they're involved in all sorts of activities. If you have elderly parents, you may end up with carer responsibilities. Point is, if you have family responsibilities there will be times when they interfere with your work commitments. If they're regular and ongoing, it's probably a good idea to discuss them with your employer and plan around them. There is no point in trying to hide them. That's a stress you don't need. Sometimes you have family emergencies and you either can't go in or you need to leave work early. You need a plan for how you're going to handle those emergencies that includes how you're going to meet any critical deadlines.

If your employer is unsympathetic to supporting you meet your family responsibilities, it may be time to find a new job or to seek help from your wider family or the community. Sometimes people only need to be asked.

The next step is to conduct a self-audit of your lifestyle choices. A self-audit can help you become aware of behaviours that may be affecting your productivity - if you're honest with yourself. Your findings will either confirm that you have no issues or that you have a few things to attend to in your own time that may help you increase your productivity.

LIFESTYLE SELF-AUDIT

This is the part where you review aspects of your lifestyle to become aware of what you're doing, or not doing, that may be causing you stress and reducing your effectiveness in the workplace. By the way, there are no right or wrong answers. What you're doing is looking at information so that you can make informed choices. Nobody is perfect at any of this stuff but the more aware you are of what you're doing, the better placed you'll be to make those informed choices that may not only improve your productivity but your lifestyle outcomes as well.

HEALTH AND FITNESS
Weight

Write down your vital statistics: age; height; weight; waist measurement. Enter 'body weight' into your search engine of choice and use one of the online calculators to determine your ideal weight, and then do some research to see what that means for you.

Record the results of your research. Remember, this document is classified: For Your Eyes Only.

Image

Take a look at your profile in the mirror the next time you're naked. What's your honest assessment:

- Trim, Taut and Terrific,
- Fat, Flabby and Floppy, or
- Somewhere in between?

Need some help deciding? Would you post that image on Facebook?

So, what's the verdict on your body weight:

- Underweight
- Within acceptable range, or
- Overweight?

And, what's the verdict on your body image:

- Terrific,
- Could use some work, or
- Could use a lot of work?

Data Analysis

Do you need to lose some weight? Do you need to get fit?

There are only two real options for addressing weight issues: changing your diet and exercise.

If you're within the acceptable weight range for your age, keep doing what you're doing. But, if you're in one of the other categories, consider making some changes to your diet and exercise regime. You might want to consult with a physician before embarking on any exercise if you've been a couch potato for a while but most of us can start simply by increasing the amount of walking we do every day.

FOOD AND OTHER THINGS YOU SWALLOW

Keep a log of what you put into your mouth for a week. Sounds pretty easy, doesn't it? But be warned, you'll probably find this more of a challenge than keeping a time log, because of the greater temptation to cheat. You need to resist that and record everything you eat, drink, or put into your mouth, including all those things that you know aren't good for you.

Buy yourself a small note book and carry it with you for the week. Write down everything you put into your mouth.

Food

- How much of what you eat is fresh food? By fresh food, let's agree we mean stuff that doesn't come in a packet, bottle, tin or plastic container.
- How much of what you eat is processed food? That's the stuff that does not meet our definition for fresh food.

Now, here's the kicker that goes with that one. What's actually in that processed food you're eating? Ever read the labels? Some of those ingredients with the fancy scientific names are there to stop the food deteriorating. Some are there simply for their taste adding features. Several of those ingredients are commonly known as sugars, which are suspected of contributing to both the obesity and type 2 diabetes epidemics sweeping the parts of the world consuming the western diet. Type 'sugar in food' into your search engine of choice to read both sides of the sugar argument, and think about how much sugar you're probably consuming without realising it.

If you're overweight, you'll need to make some changes to your diet if you want to lose weight and feel more energetic. The weight loss mantra used to be: eat less, walk more. If you take a look at what they're saying these days, it's not so much about eating less but eating consciously or being more aware of what you're actually putting into your body.

If you need to make changes to your diet, don't go on a diet. You'll be better off if you make some informed choices about what you eat, and decide to make a lifestyle change to eating healthier food, and not a short-term effort to lose weight.

Data analysis

Do you need to make some changes?

Brain chemistry

- How much alcohol are you consuming daily? Weekly?
- What other substances are you putting into your system that mess with your brain chemistry?
- Despite all the health warnings, are you still smoking?

If you're consuming substances like alcohol and drugs that mess with your brain chemistry, there really are only two viable options if you want to increase your productivity: abstinence and moderation.

If you're taking recreational drugs or dabbling in narcotics, you might want to ask yourself why and spend some time with your answer or excuse.

There are other ways of coping with stress that don't mess with your brain chemistry. One way is meditation. Another is running. You don't have to poison yourself. You have choices.

Data analysis

Do you need to make some changes?

CURRENT PRIORITIES

One way of working out your current priorities is to find out how you spend your time. To do that, keep a time log for a week. Simply record the time you spend doing whatever it is you do. For reference, there are 168 hours in a week. If you want more data to get a better idea of your pattern, keep a log for a 4-week period - that's 672 hours.

Data analysis

Transfer the data from your time log to a table like the example below.

Activity	Hours per week	% of total hours
Working		
Watching television		
Sleeping		
Exercising or playing sport		
Meeting family responsibilities		
Reading or studying		
Meditating or sitting quietly doing nothing		
Doing fun things with family and friends		
Being with your significant other		
Being with your children		

Construct a timetable to illustrate your daily, weekly, and monthly time use patterns. One easy way to do that is to transfer your time log data into a spreadsheet and color code it.

It's important to look at your totals and your patterns.

- Do you work seven days a week?
- When do you get up and when do you go to bed?
- Are you doing any exercise?

If you get 56 hours of sleep in a week, there is a difference between getting 8 hours a night every night and 20 hours on the weekend with only 5 hours a night during the week. There is also a difference between getting 5 hours a night and 5 hours of interrupted sleep a night. Ask any nursing mother or a soldier that's been on active duty.

If you read anything on sleep, the advice you usually see is to get regular sleep.

Are you spending any time meditating or sitting quietly doing nothing? If you're not giving yourself any regular downtime, I suggest you read *The Pause Principle* by Kevin Cashman, especially if you're a leader in the workplace.

This may not be in your data but when was the last time you took a vacation, that is, took time off from work?

When you look at your data, what does it tell you about your current priorities? Do you think you might need to make some changes?

One thing to keep in mind is that you don't necessarily become more productive by spending more time at work. Counterintuitive as it may seem, establishing balance in your life is more effective for increasing your productivity - both at home and in the workplace.

MONEY MATTERS

I assume you know how much you earn each month, but do you know how much you're spending?

No, I'm not going to ask you to keep a spending log but I am suggesting that you invest the time required to get a firm understanding of your current cash flow situation. However, if you find that you can't account for a significant amount of your spending, then you might want to keep a spending log for a week or more to see where those missing dollars, pounds or euros are going.

This is an exercise that is best completed using a spreadsheet but it can be done on a sheet of paper with the aid of a calculator.

What you need to complete this exercise is a copy of the accounts that you pay and your bank account statements, and I recommend that you do it for a complete financial or calendar year.

If you are an employee, use your net income; that is, the amount you actually receive from your employer - that's the amount you're trying to live on.

If you're self-employed, use your gross income. Taxes and levies are expenses you need to allow for each month. Even if you only pay them quarterly or annually, you need to have the cash to do that at the time. You also need to account for your business expenses as well as your personal expenses, and know the difference between the two if you want to avoid disputes with the tax authorities.

Draw up a table with months across the top and a list of income and expenses down the left-hand side, as in the example on page 18.

Group your personal expenses into two categories: essential and discretionary.

Essential expenses are the things required for survival; like food, water, housing, electricity and clothing.

Discretionary expenses are not related to survival. They're expenses you have a choice about, things like going to the movies, eating out, another pair of shoes, cigarettes and life insurance.

Some of your expenses will be regular in the sense that you need to pay them every month or quarter. For example, expenses like rent or mortgage payments are usually both fixed in amount and regular in frequency of payment. Food and utility payments, on the other hand, may be regular in frequency of payment but variable in amount. Other items, like car expenses, may vary both in frequency and amount.

How many credit cards are there in your household? Remember, if you pay for an item with a credit card, it's still an expense, and if you don't pay it off it becomes a debt with an interest expense attached.

To keep things simple, I suggest you create an expense called 'petty cash' as a catch all for the money you spend on low value items like coffee and lunch during the month. The important point is to get it as accurate as you can without stressing over every dollar, pound or euro.

Income/Expense	Jan	Feb	Mar	Apr	May	Jun	Jul	Aug	Sep	Oct	Nov	Dec	Total
Income 1													
Income 2													
Total Income													
Essentials Expenses													
Rent/Mortgage													
Food													
Total													
Discretionary Expenses													
Entertainment													
Booze													
Cigarettes													
Petty cash													
Total													
Total Expenses													
Cash flow													

Data analysis

When you have filled in the table, total your expenses for each month. Then, for each month, subtract your total expenses amount from your total income amount, and record the result in a separate row labelled cash flow. If you used a spreadsheet, you might want to graph that result. It's also valuable to compare the annual total of your expenses with your total income for the year.

- If your annual expenses equal your annual income, you're spending everything you earn. You need to do something if you want to reduce your monetary stress level.
- If your annual expenses exceed your annual income, you're spending more than you earn. You definitely need to do something to reduce your monetary stress level.

If you have credit cards and you can't clear the debt in a particular month, you spent more in that month than you earned. If you have rolling credit card debt, which you never seem to be able to pay off, you're continually spending more than you earn.

In the final analysis, if you need to do something, there are only two things you can do: earn more income or spend less money. If spending less is your only viable option, you need to draw up a plan - also known as a budget – to control your discretionary spending and reduce your debts, and apply self-discipline.

RELATIONSHIPS
Relationship with your significant other

We all want to be loved but sometimes we mess up our relationships with the people we love the most. We get our priorities out of alignment. We take each other for granted and wake up to a different reality than the one we thought we were living.

How's your relationship going with your significant other?

- Are you spending quality time together?
- Are you fighting or arguing?
- Are you on good speaking terms or giving each other the silent treatment?
- Are you being abused physically, emotionally or mentally? Are you the one doing the abusing?
- If you're away from home a lot, how are you keeping the flame alive?
- Do you know what's going on in your partner's life?

They might be tough questions but it's tough trying to be productive at work when you're living with relationship stress.

What overall rating would you give the relationship with your current significant other:

- Good
- Bad, or
- Indifferent?

Only you know the answer to that question but you need to be honest with yourself. It's easy to delude yourself that things are better than they are.

If you identify issues, remember that there is plenty of professional help available if you want it. If it's really bad, maybe you need to consider whether you want to stay in the relationship.

Relationships with your children

- How much time are you spending with your children?
- Do you know what's going on in their lives?

This is not an area you can afford to let slide. Don't kid yourself that you're doing it all for them if they never see you. They won't thank you. They want your presence more than anything else you can provide.

Data analysis

Are there things you could work on with your partner to improve your relationship? Are there behaviours you need to change? Do you need to ask for help or can work it out with your partner? What about with your children?

No significant other

If your relationship stress comes from not having a significant other in your life, take a look at your time log.

What's your current focus?

- Is there room in your life for a partner at the moment?
- Do you want to make room?
- What stories are you telling yourself about relationships?

Data analysis

If you're blocking what you tell yourself you want by not being available for a relationship to develop, consider making time in your life for a partner.

If you're telling yourself that you're not good enough or that you'll never find someone to love you, it might be time to change your story.

If you want to do something about attracting someone into your life, I suggest you start by reading *Calling in the One* by Katherine Woodward Thomas.

FAMILY RESPONSIBILITIES

Do you have any specific family responsibilities that impact on your workplace productivity?

For example:

- If you have young children, do you look after them when they're sick or on school holidays?
- Do you have a partner with a chronic illness or other health issues?
- Do you have a role in caring for elderly parents?

Data analysis

The point in identifying your responsibilities is to consider whether you have a plan in place to deal with things like medical emergencies or carer responsibilities, or not. For example, do you share the responsibilities with your partner? Or your siblings? Have you looked at working from home as a viable option when you can't make it into work?

Now that you've completed a Lifestyle Self-Audit, it's time to consider an action plan to address the issues you identified.

LIFESTYLE ACTION PLAN

An action plan is a list of activities designed to take you from where you are to where you want to be. The important part, however, comes after you draw up the plan. Unless you take the actions described in your action plan, it will be nothing more than a well-intentioned list.

HEALTH AND FITNESS

Write down the steps you intend to take to either maintain or improve your current level of health and fitness.

Exercise

Be as realistic as possible. If you need to lose some weight, by all means set yourself a weight goal but don't kid yourself you can do it in a few weeks. Go back and read some of those sites you found searching online for 'body weight' to help you work out a realistic time frame. If it's a long time since you exercised regularly, start with walking for ten minutes a day instead of rushing off and joining the gym. We're talking about establishing new habits. They take time.

Action steps:

Eating

If you don't do the cooking in your household, discuss your plans with the cook. If you eat out or buy fast food all the time, consider learning to cook or reverting to home cooked meals. Do some research online to get an understanding of what healthy eating looks like. Hint: fresh food figures in it a lot. If you have no idea when it comes to cooking, let me suggest a little book I wrote for guys living alone: *Cooking 4 One*. It's about the basic processes. Cooking is not that difficult but, again, it's a choice.

Action steps:

Looking after your brain chemistry

- **Alcohol**
- **Recreational drugs**
- **Narcotics**
- **Medicines**

If you want to be productive, it's not going to happen while you're abusing your brain.

If you need to take action to address substance abuse, it will not be easy, and you will need to be honest enough with yourself to seek help.

Action steps:

Cigarettes

If you want to give up smoking, type 'smoking consciously' into your search engine of choice for information on how you can quit.

Action steps:

MONEY

Write down the steps you intend to take to get your cash flow under control. At the very least, draw up a budget and decide what you will be spending your money on before you spend it. This is the reverse of the cash flow exercise you did.

Spending

Consider limiting your spending to 80% of your income.

If you live in a two-income household, this step cannot be done alone. Before you start, discuss your money situation with your partner and work towards an agreed outcome. Once you have agreement, focus on reducing your discretionary spending to free up the cash required to reduce outstanding credit card debts.

When you have cleared your credit cards, start on a savings plan so that you'll have the cash to pay for those discretionary items when you want to buy them.

Changing your eating habits might also help you save money, especially if you have been eating out a lot. Going home instead of going to those after work happy hours will also contribute some extra dollars to your bottom line. Getting control of your cash flow requires self-discipline, and a preparedness to start over if you slip up. And, be realistic; allocate yourself or each partner an allowance to spend without having to account for it.

Income

The other side of the money equation is income. Can you get a better paying job? Can you earn more in your current job by being more productive?

Is there a way you could earn some extra income on the side? If you have skills to share, consider offering a course on a site like Skillshare.com. The opportunities are out there.

Action steps:

REBALANCING PRIORITIES

Write down the steps you intend to take to get your life into balance.

It's not uncommon for people focused on productivity in the workplace to find, when they look at the way they are allocating their time, that their lives are out of balance. Usually the problem is too great a focus on work at the expense of other areas in their lives.

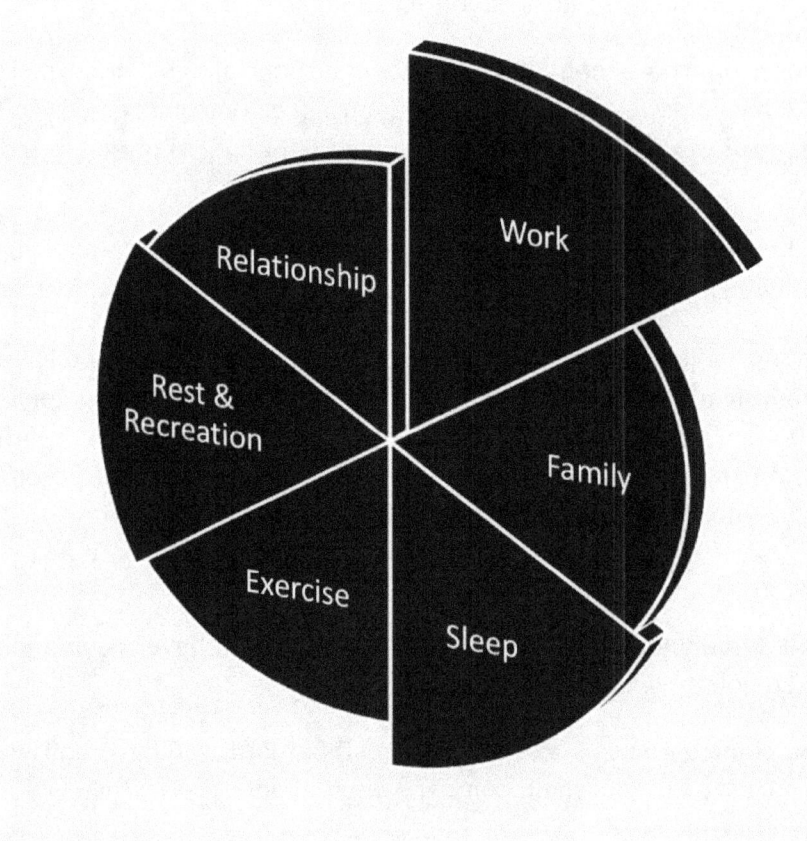

If you picture the aspects of your life as making up the components of a wheel, the aim is to get all things into alignment so that your wheel will turn smoothly. Interestingly, getting things into balance actually makes it easier to be more productive at work.

If you need some ideas for rebalancing your life, consider *How to Live a Good Life* by Jonathan Fields.

Action steps:

Relationships

Think about this as you consider how you're going to rebalance things in your life.

Significant other

Write down the steps you intend to take to maintain or improve the quality of your relationship with your significant other.

If you're at the point where ending the relationship is your best option, then research the steps you need to take to do that and seek appropriate legal advice, especially if you're ending a long-term relationship or there are children involved.

If you're looking to attract a significant other into your life, remember to consider *Calling in the One* by Katherine Woodward Thomas.

Action steps:

Children

Write down the steps you intend to take to maintain or improve the quality of your relationship with your children.

Action steps:

FAMILY RESPONSIBILITIES

Write down your plan of action for dealing with any family responsibilities that need to be balanced with working.

Action steps:

Now that you've drawn up your Lifestyle Action Plan, make a commitment to act on it. Go to your calendar and set up a monthly review date, just like you would for any other project, and regularly review your progress and update your plan.

ATTITUDE

No-one dictates the attitude or mindset you take to work with you. Your attitude is one of those things you have total control over.

Unsurprisingly, the attitude you take to work with you influences your productivity, and you don't need to read a stack of research papers to realise that you'll be more productive if you enjoy your job and approach your work with a positive mental attitude.

Let's start by addressing: 'I hate my job.'

There's plenty of research out there telling us that we hate our jobs. You'd be forgiven for thinking it was a modern-day epidemic, but I suspect things have always been that way. I don't imagine, for example, that Roman soldiers stationed on Hadrian's Wall at the edge of their empire enjoyed their jobs during the winter any more than you would in their place.

Although you might have any number of valid reasons for hating your job, you're not going to be either happy or productive while you do.

We live in a society where money is the medium of exchange, so we need access to money. There's no denying that fact. For most of us, working either for ourselves or someone else is how we get that access. So, whether you hate your job or not, you need to have one until you establish a level of financial freedom that will allow you to leave your job. For most of us, that takes about forty years, if we save for our retirement through established vehicles like social security or superannuation. That's a long time to hate your job.

Hating your job is an attitude, which means you can change your mind about it

It's a lot easier for most of us to change our minds than it is to change our jobs, especially if we want to do something about enjoying life while we are at work.

It's easy to focus on things that you don't like about your job but that's not helpful if you want to be happier and more productive. Instead of complaining about how terrible things are, consider the following:

- Revisit your purpose for going to work and relegate earning money to being one of the outcomes of working, instead of making it the reason why you work.
- Identify what it is that you do while you are at work. Focus on getting enjoyment or fulfilment from doing that well.
- Identify an aspect of your work that you appreciate. Focus on that.

- Be noticed for the right reasons. Become the best at whatever it is that you do. Be the friendly one, the helpful one, the one who puts the service into customer service.
- Watch your self-talk. Pay attention to what you tell yourself about your job, and what you tell others about it.
- Be thankful that you have a job to complain about, and stop complaining about it.

One useful strategy is to treat work as a game. When you see it as a game, it's easier to not take things so seriously and to allow yourself to have some fun when you're at work.

By all means, if there is nothing about your current job that you can like, start looking for another one, but don't put off addressing your attitude to work. At some point, you need to take responsibility for how you present yourself in the workplace: as someone who wants to contribute or as someone who thinks they're entitled to a free ride. It's a lot easier to be productive when you're a contributor.

Being passionate about your job helps but it may not be enough

Being passionate about your job makes it a lot easier to get up and go to work every morning but it doesn't guarantee that you'll be productive. You can get stuck in seeing things a certain way or happily go along with the way things have always been done. You can fall into a routine that keeps you busy but not necessarily productive. It is, however, a lot easier to become more productive if you enjoy what you're doing and believe that you're making a difference.

Developing a productive mindset

If you want to be productive at work, you need a productive mindset or the attitude that you are there to not only work but to give it your best shot. This attitude comes naturally to some people. The rest of us can adopt it and then apply it. In the final analysis, your attitude to work is a choice you make.

Productive attitude indicators

Whether you're employed or self-employed, there are some ways of approaching your work that simply make you more productive. Productive people:

- have a 'can do' attitude and look for ways to do things more effectively. They're the ones looking for ways to work smarter instead of harder. The ones asking; why?
- accept responsibility for getting things done. They deliver on their promises to customers and co-workers. They don't make excuses or palm tasks off to others. They follow through to ensure the job is done.
- are leaders even if that word does not appear in their title. They do the right thing even when nobody else is looking. They set the standard for professional behaviour.

- understand that they're there to contribute and not just to pass the time. They're the ones putting in the honest day's effort, the ones fulfilling their part of their employment contract or service commitment.
- are there to help. They're at work to make a difference.
- are open to change. They embrace new ways of doing things and help others to cope with new systems and expectations.
- believe in themselves and their abilities. They know they can get the job done and they ask for help when they need it.
- are prepared to get their hands dirty to get the job done. They are the ones in the arena participating, not the ones standing around complaining.

The next step is to conduct a self-audit of the attitude you take to work with you. A self-audit can help you become aware of attitudes that may be influencing your productivity - if you're honest with yourself. Your findings will either confirm that you have no issues or that you have a few things to attend to that may help you increase your productivity.

ATTITUDE SELF-AUDIT

This is the part where you review your attitude in the workplace to see whether it's facilitating or impeding your productivity. The good part about attitude is that it is not set in concrete but, like everything else, if you are not aware of your attitude or how it could be affecting your workplace productivity, you can't do anything about it.

RATE YOUR ATTITUDE TO YOUR JOB
- I enjoy it
- It's sort of okay
- I hate it.

Think about what your answer means, especially if you picked: I hate my job.

If you really hate your job, what are your options? For example, do you need to get serious about finding another job?

What if there are no other jobs available for you to go to?

You could just quit, but that decision may have consequences you're not prepared to live with. Also, keep in mind that your attitude to your job may not be dependent on your job but on how you think about it.

If quitting isn't the answer, what is?

What could you do to shift your rating from 'I hate my job' to 'It's sort of okay'?

If you rated your attitude as 'It's sort of okay', what could you do to move your rating to 'I enjoy my job'?

YOUR WORK

Describe what you do when you are at work or make a list of the tasks you perform at work.

Is there anything that you do that you are particularly good at or could become good at if you applied yourself to mastering that task?

Don't limit yourself to just one thing. Being multi-skilled makes you more valuable to your employer, even if you work for yourself.

THINGS YOU APPRECIATE ABOUT YOUR WORK

Make a list of at least five things you appreciate about your work. Don't stop at five if you can list more.

TALKING ABOUT YOUR WORK

Listen to your self-talk. What are you telling yourself about your work?

Remember, if you repeat something often enough you'll believe it's true even if it's total bullshit, and no-one repeats stuff to you more than you do.

What do you tell other people about your work?

If you're having trouble with this one, ask your partner or your friends to reflect some of it back for you.

When you're analysing what you say, notice what you are actually saying about yourself within the context of your work. Are you running yourself down?

MY PRODUCTIVE ATTITUDE INDICATORS

Identify the things that make you productive, for example:

- I have a 'can do' attitude.
- I look for ways to do things more effectively.
- I accept responsibility for getting things done.
- I deliver on my promises.
- I do the right thing even when no-one is looking.
- I put in an honest day's effort.
- I help others.
- I'm friendly
- I treat people with respect.
- I'm at work to contribute.
- I'm committed to making a difference.
- I'm open to change.
- I believe I can do the job.
- I ask for help when I need it.
- I get the job done.
- I don't wait around; I make things happen.

Data analysis

Do you think you have a productive mindset or do you need to work on developing one?

Now that you've completed an Attitude Self-Audit, it's time to consider an action plan to address the issues you identified.

ATTITUDE ACTION PLAN

An action plan is a list of activities designed to take you from where you are to where you want to be. The important part, however, comes after you draw up the plan. Unless you take the actions described in your action plan, it will be nothing more than a well-intentioned list.

YOUR ATTITUDE TO YOUR JOB

If you answered: I enjoy my job

Write down what you plan to do to maintain that attitude.

If you answered: It's sort of okay

Write down what you plan to do to shift your attitude to: I enjoy my job.

If you answered: I hate my job

Write down what you plan to do to shift your attitude to: It's sort of okay.

If your plan is to find a new job, write down the actions you will take to find and apply for a new job. Be specific, but have an action plan for what you'll do at work while you're looking for that new job or if you can't find one.

If your plan is to change your attitude instead of changing your job, describe how you are going to work on doing that. For example, you could start by reading *Change Your Thoughts, Change Your Life* by Wayne Dyer.

Action steps:

YOUR WORK

This is where you choose to focus on getting enjoyment or fulfilment from doing things well, and take a small step that will give your work a specific purpose every day. It's also a way of making yourself more valuable to your employer.

Refer to your list of tasks and select one or more of them to concentrate on mastering, and describe the action steps you plan to take to acquire that mastery.

Action steps:

Things to appreciate about your work

One way of building a positive attitude to your work is to appreciate it, or aspects of it.

Find ways to remind yourself of the things you appreciate about your job. For example, store a copy of the list on your smartphone and read it before you go to work.

Action steps:

Talking about your work

Don't be surprised if you discovered that you say a lot of negative things about your work, and yourself within the context of your work. Become aware that you might be telling yourself lies based on your interpretation of events and not the cold hard facts. The next time you catch yourself doing it, ask to see the evidence for your statement. Look for facts, not opinion. Often, it's our own opinions that are misinformed or distorted. Hard to swallow, I know, but true, nevertheless.

Write out some positive things you can say about your work and yourself instead of those negative things you have been saying, and practise saying them to yourself. This is a technique known as reframing. Type that term into your search engine of choice to find out more about how you can do it from the experts.

Action steps:

PRODUCTIVE MINDSET

Do you have a productive mindset or do you need to work on developing one?

Refer to your productive attitude indicators and write down the action steps you plan to take to develop a more productive mindset.

Action steps:

Now that you've drawn up your Attitude Action Plan, make a commitment to act on it. Go to your calendar and set up a monthly review date, just like you would for any other project, and regularly review your progress and update your plan.

Work environment

There are two aspects to any work environment: physical and cultural.

Physical

The physical refers to where you actually work, whether it's a shop floor, a street, a retail outlet, a classroom, or a corner office. It includes the tools you work with to deliver whatever goods or services you provide, things like desktop computers, specialised machinery, patrol cars, and retail counters; and the actual conditions under which you work, for example, noise, temperature, weather, proximity of other workers, lighting and access to fresh air.

The properties of your work environment are generally dictated by your profession or occupation and, unless you are self-employed, by your employer's preferences or budget. If you are self-employed, you can choose to set up your workplace to support your productivity. For example, you can buy new equipment, change the settings on the thermostat, open the windows or upgrade the light bulbs. On the other hand, if you are an employee, you usually need to make the most of where you are with the equipment available to be productive.

The good thing about the physical aspect of your work environment is that it's a known quantity that doesn't change from day to day or even from year to year, so you can plan around it. You can either use the physical conditions in your workplace as an excuse for doing nothing differently or the reason for doing something to make you more productive.

Setting up your workspace to help you do your job correctly is one way of working smarter.

I worked in office environments for many years. One job I had in banking was in a centralised loan approvals department. Loan applications arrived from the bank's branches inside specially designed envelopes we called packets. They looked impressive but they also all looked the same, except for the applicants' names written in bold letters in the top left hand corner. And, of course, the contents on one packet looked much like the contents of any other packet. To make matters worse, the lending officers continually telephoned to check on the progress of their applications. (We eventually overcame that problem and increased our productivity by adding a loan tracking module to the lending system, for which I got to write the operating procedures - my first writing job.)

When I joined that department, I learnt very quickly that you needed an organised desktop if you were going to find the right packet whenever anyone rang, and more importantly, you needed to make sure you didn't mix up the contents of different packets.

Several years later, when I worked in lending administration, I often found that errors in the way an account had been set up were related to the loan packet containing material from another application.

Being productive can be as simple as being attentive to the task so that you do it right the first time and don't create unnecessary work for someone else. Being productive doesn't necessarily mean being the fastest operator - but you will be quicker if you know where your tools are and can access them with ease.

CULTURAL

You've probably come across the term corporate culture. It's worth dropping that term into your search engine of choice to get an overview of the types of cultures people claim to see in the business world.

For our purposes, let's agree that corporate culture is the way people within a workplace behave.

Most employers have behavioural expectations of their employees. Some of those expectations are written into formal codes of conduct, vision statements and employee handbooks. In government organisations, they might even be written into law. Others are unwritten and often unspoken assumptions or beliefs that evolve over time about the way things should be done.

Interestingly, the description of any workplace culture is dependent upon the perspective of the person doing the describing, and a firm's view of itself does not necessarily align with either the view of its employees or its customers.

In my experience, organisations often have unspoken rules of engagement between employees and management, which are often nothing more than ways of maintaining the power equations within an organisation, and it's not uncommon for employees and managers to have different understandings of those rules.

The culture of a workplace will either foster or block intentions for improving productivity

In a workplace that embraces and encourages innovation, you will probably encounter support for any innovative ideas you promote. People will allow you to experiment and try new things, and it will be easier to get people to adopt new ways of doing things, despite the fact that people everywhere are initially resistant to change.

In a workplace that trusts its employees, it's easy to 'manage up', that is, persuade your manager to see the value of doing something differently. But, it's almost impossible for ideas from the shop-floor to go anywhere in a firm where management believes that it, and only it, knows best.

A word of warning

As you work on your productivity, be aware that there are people within your workplace that will see you as a threat when you make a move to increase your productivity. Your managers may appreciate your efforts, especially if you're making them look good, but your co-workers may not be happy with you for showing them up as being inefficient or needing to change the way they do things.

It's a sad fact of life that sometimes you need to change your friends to get on in the world, even after you have shared your shortcuts and ways of working smarter with them. Some people just don't want to be more productive.

The next step is to conduct a self-audit of your work environment to identify how to make the most of the physical aspects of your workplace, and to increase your awareness of the corporate culture within which you work. Your findings will help you to develop an action plan for increasing your productivity with as much support as possible.

WORK ENVIRONMENT SELF-AUDIT

This is the part where you review your work environment to see whether it's facilitating or impeding your productivity. The point of this exercise is to identify the things you have control over in your physical workspace, and to become aware of the cultural context within which you work.

YOUR IMMEDIATE WORKSPACE

Your workspace is usually the one part of your work environment that you exercise some control over, and knowing where your tools are so that you can access them with ease is just as important as having them. Take a good look at your immediate workspace. Is it set up to help you do your job correctly?

Things you can change versus things you can't in your physical environment

Identify the things you can change to improve your immediate workspace, and the things you might be able to persuade your employer to change to improve your physical working conditions. Focus on those.

Identify the things you can't change and don't waste your time and energy on them.

Productivity is better served by working on the things you have control over or that you can influence.

Ergonomics

Ergonomics is about designing and arranging things for human use. You can get the full story by entering ergonomics into your search engine of choice. This is an especially important topic for people who work in offices with computers. It deals with the design and set up of chairs and desks, and the placement of computers, keyboards and mice. If you work for a large organisation you will probably know about ergonomics and how to set up your workstation to minimise injuries like lower back pain, tension in your shoulders, deep vein thrombosis, repetitive use injuries and eye strain.

If you know about ergonomics, have you actually taken the information seriously and set up your workspace to support your body while you are doing your job?

If you work for yourself or a smaller employer and haven't heard about ergonomics, look after your body by looking it up and adjusting your workspace accordingly.

By the way, it doesn't only apply to people sitting at desks.

Safety equipment

What's your attitude to safety equipment?

There is always a good reason for using safety equipment, for example, protecting your hearing, eyesight or body parts. Although it's tempting not to use it, especially when you think you can do things quicker or easier without it, that decision is definitely counterproductive when you need its protection. The productive option is to use it every time.

Make a list of the safety equipment provided by your employer or recommended for people in your profession or trade. Do you use it? Do you need to find out how it works? Does it work or does it need to be replaced or updated? Do you need an attitude adjustment?

Distractions

If you work with a computer, you know it can be a source of distraction, especially if it's connected to the internet. Spend some time exploring how notifications and alerts operate on your computer. Find out how you can turn them off either temporarily or permanently. If, like me, you work on a Mac, the thing to look for is the 'Do Not Disturb' setting in the Notification Centre. Switching that setting on stops notifications from interrupting your train of thought but keeps them in a spot where you can read them when you're ready. Windows now has an Action Centre that stores notifications, and the trick is to turn it on, if you want to stop all those annoying pop up notifications. Plenty of guidance out there on the internet if you need help with that.

Does your workplace have other sources of distraction, like noise?

YOUR WORKPLACE CULTURE

How old is the culture in your workplace? Are you working in the twenty-first century yet?

The last place I worked, The Australian Taxation Office (ATO), has a one hundred year plus history and has reinvented itself several times, yet, when I left in 2015, the ATO was two years into a program called 'Reinventing the ATO' that was all about refreshing its corporate culture and bringing its workforce into the twenty-first century. It was a great opportunity for people like me, who were interested in changing the way things were done. It was very stressful for others, especially those who liked the structure and order of the old way of doing things.

If you want to increase your productivity or work smarter, you need to be aware of the culture in your workplace because, sometimes, you will be supported and, sometimes, you won't. So, what's it like in your workplace?

- What are the rules where you work? Are they written or unspoken? Can you question them? Does anybody follow them? What happens when you break one?
- Are you encouraged to innovate or simply to follow the rules and ask no questions?
- What happens when you suggest a change to a process or a procedure?
- Do people 'walk the talk' or say one thing and do another?

- Is your workplace a safe place? Can you be yourself there or are you expected to conform?
- Can you take an idea to your manager or boss or do you have to wait for someone higher up the corporate ladder to have an idea before anything gets changed?
- How do your co-workers or colleagues respond when you suggest doing something different?
- Do you and your team talk about how you do things on a regular basis?

You can be productive in any workplace culture, but in some you need to be aware of what the rules are so you can play the game without getting hurt.

Now that you've completed a Work Environment Self-Audit, it's time to consider an action plan to address the issues you identified.

WORK ENVIRONMENT ACTION PLAN

An action plan is a list of activities designed to take you from where you are to where you want to be. The important part, however, comes after you draw up the plan. Unless you take the actions described in your action plan, it will be nothing more than a well-intentioned list.

YOUR IMMEDIATE WORKSPACE

Things you can change versus things you can't in your physical environment

List the things you can change to improve your immediate workspace, and the things you might be able to persuade your employer to change to improve your physical working conditions. Focus on those. What changes do you intend to make or request?

Action steps:

Ergonomics

Detail any changes you need to make to your workspace to apply what you know about ergonomics.

If your employer provides an ergonomic assessment, do you need to arrange one?

If you're self-employed, do you need to consider buying some new equipment?

Action steps:

Safety equipment

Review the list of the safety equipment provided by your employer or recommended for people in your profession or trade. List any steps you need to take to receive the protection of using that equipment.

Action steps:

Distractions

Computer notifications. Do you know how to turn off unwanted notifications and alerts?

If your workplace has other sources of distraction, like noise, identify what action you can take, for example, using earplugs, to minimise them.

Action steps:

YOUR WORKPLACE CULTURE

Remember, you can be productive in any workplace culture.

Identify some strategies you can adopt to enhance your productivity within the existing culture. In other words, decide how you can play within the rules. For example, change your attitude to work, become a standard setter, use existing pathways to promote new ideas or network with others inside the firm.

Determine if there are any actions you can take to influence your workplace culture. For example, speaking up in meetings, proposing new ways of doing things, networking, accepting opportunities to work with others on change projects.

Action steps:

Now that you've drawn up your Workplace Environment Action Plan, make a commitment to act on it. Go to your calendar and set up a monthly review date, just like you would for any other project, and regularly review your progress and update your plan.

Habits

A habit is an automated action or response. You deploy habits everywhere - not just in the workplace. That's one reason why I started with lifestyle. You need to be consciously aware of your habits to increase your productivity.

The automation feature of the human brain allows you to perform complex tasks, like driving or typing, without much conscious effort after an initial period of deliberate practice. The repetition involved in mastering complex tasks installs routines into your personal operating system - the subconscious mind. Those routines require little conscious attention until you need to update them when, for example, you buy a new car or smartphone. Automated actions enhance productivity.

Habitual behaviours are automated responses to circumstances or other people's behaviours, or simply ways you go about doing things. For example, driving the same way to work every day, buying the same thing for lunch, always going to Friday night drinks. They also include getting angry when someone disagrees with your opinion, always deferring to the opinions of authority figures, or not listening when someone is talking to you. The challenge with habitual behaviours is becoming aware that you are operating from habit and not from conscious choice. If that's not scary enough, you also have habitual ways of thinking that are based on your beliefs, which are based on your experiences, and these can get you into trouble.

Habits can be useful but they can also be a curse, especially when you get stuck doing the same thing over and over when circumstances have changed.

Fortunately, by becoming aware of your habits you can do something about them and replace outmoded ones with new ones. Two books I have found useful for identifying and changing habits are: *Liminal Thinking* by Dave Gray, and *Think or Swim: The One Choice That Changes Everything* by Gina Millicone-Long. My favourite tool from Gina's book is the 42-day projects practice, which Gina created in response to that famous answer to the meaning of life question in *The Hitchhiker's Guide to the Galaxy*. It works for me; it's a great tool for updating your habits.

The next step is to conduct a self-audit of your habits. A self-audit will help you identify any habitual behaviours or ways of thinking that are affecting your productivity. Your findings will help you to develop an action plan to upgrade, replace or delete those parts of the subconscious operating system underpinning your productivity.

Habits Self-Audit

This is the part where you review your habits to see whether they're facilitating or impeding your productivity. The point of the exercise is not to make you feel bad about your habits. After all, many of your habits are useful. The point is to become aware of your habits. You can't do anything about a habit unless you know you have it, and then you can decide to drop it, change it or replace it so that it serves you.

Starting your day

How do you start your day? This is really a two-part question.

1. How do you start your day when you wake up at home?
2. How do you start your day when you get to work?

Describe your morning routine at home

What do you do from the time you wake up until you leave for work?

You might not think that you have a morning routine but, when you take the time to notice, you'll probably be surprised at how regular your mornings are. The way you start your day usually involves a string of habitual behaviours you don't think about. You simply get up and do them. The downside of not thinking about what you do every morning is getting the same outcome day after day: always running late or always on time.

Describe your morning routine at work

What do you do to start your day at work?

Take the time to observe what you do as you start your day over the course of a week and write it down.

Data analysis

Now that you have a record of how you start your day, it's time to think about how your morning routine might be affecting your productivity.

- Are you creating stress for yourself by sleeping in? Or are you an early bird?
- Do you eat breakfast? At home? On the run? At your desk at work?
- Do you drive the car when you could take public transport? Why do you do that?
- Do you take any time to set up your day? Do you use a to do list? Do you set priorities?
- Do you waste half an hour having coffee and socialising before you settle down to the task?
- Are your morning routines contributing to your productivity or getting in the way?

If you need help sorting out a morning routine that will set you up for a productive day, take a look at *Miracle Morning* by Hal Elrod and *18 Minutes* by Peter Bregman. Hal can help you get your day started constructively at home. Peter can help you start your day at work so that you get the most out of being there.

DOING THE JOB

Your job may sound exciting to outsiders but, in reality, it will involve a lot of routine. Even creative activities have a fair amount of routine in them. For example, being a writer requires daily writing activity, being a musician requires daily practice, and working in an office involves a lot of repetitive tasks on computers.

If you're doing the same thing day after day, it's fairly easy to fall into habitual routines. In some instances, that's not a bad strategy, but in others it can be counterproductive.

The danger with habitual routines is you can easily become inattentive - and that's when you fail to notice mistakes or any changes that require a different response from normal. This is a particular risk if you work in an organisation that insists on tasks being completed according to standard procedures.

The benefit of habitual routines is they can get you into the zone where you do your best work.

To make the most of your habitual workplace behaviours to boost your productivity, you first need to be aware of your current habits, and to make the conscious decision to change them, or develop new ones, if required.

A few questions to help you review your habits at work.

Structure

- How do you structure your day? Do you do the same task all day or do you do different tasks at different times of the day?
- Do you have any control over what you do, and when you do it?
- Do you have control over how you do it?
- Do you ever try ways of doing a task differently?
- Are you ever required to think about what you're doing?

Breaks

- Do you take a break every hour or do you work for hours on end?
- Do you leave your workplace and go outside for lunch? Do you leave your desk?

Email

- Do you respond to every email when it arrives?
- Do you devote a specific time to answering incoming emails?
- Do you pause and review what you have written before hitting send?
- Do you plan your email messages?
- Do you use email to avoid speaking to people directly?

Telephone

- Do you answer every call or do you let some go through to voice mail?
- Do you manage your incoming calls or let them manage you?
- Do you plan the content of your telephone calls before you make them?
- Do you pay attention during teleconferences or use that time for other things?

Meetings

- Do you accept every meeting invitation?
- Do you prepare for meetings or simply attend?
- Do you participate or simply listen or let your mind wander?

Collaboration

- Do you seek help when you need it?
- Do you share ideas with others? Or do you keep things to yourself?
- Do you understand that collaboration is working with others?

Communication

- Do you listen when others are speaking or do you interrupt?
- Do you like the sound of your own voice? Are you a windbag?
- Do you check that others have understood your requests?
- Do you confirm that you have understood what has been asked?
- Do you prepare and review your message or response before communicating it?

Data analysis

Take a look at your answers.

- Are your habitual routines or work habits helpful or are they stifling your efforts to be more productive?
- Are there alternative ways of setting up your day to break up those routines? For example, can you rotate tasks with your colleagues?
- If you do the same thing all day every day, can you build in some breaks? A coffee break? A study break? A meeting or a workshop? A game? Taking a break sounds counterintuitive but it works. You'll be more productive if you give your brain a break every hour or so.
- If you do a variety of tasks, when is the best time in your day for completing different types of tasks? For example, are you a morning person who does your best creative work first thing or do need to do some routine administrative tasks for a few hours before you're ready to be creative?
- Do you need to change any of your behaviours in order to be more productive?

Sometimes, it's as easy as pausing and thinking about what you're about to do or say. Sometimes, you need to rethink the way you normally do things.

ENDING YOUR DAY

How do you end your day? This is another two-part question.

1. How do you end your day at work?
2. How do you end your day at home?

Describe how you end your day at work

What do you do when it's time to pack up and go home?

Take the time to observe what you do as you end your day over the course of a week and write it down.

Describe how you end your day at home

How do you spend those last few hours of your day before you go to bed? Do you do the same thing every night? Are you a night owl?

Data analysis

Take a look at your answers.

- Do you simply pack up and head for the door at the end of your work day, or do you take a moment to see whether you achieved what you had planned for the day and to plan for the next work day?
- Are you driven by the clock or whether you achieved what you had planned? Do you leave at the same time every day? Are you the first or last to leave? Do you stay back until you've finished what you had planned or agreed to do that day?
- When you get home from work, do you do anything to de-stress from your working day? For example, do you meditate, read, exercise or do you have a drink?
- Do you stay up late watching TV, surfing the net or posting on social media? Or do you give yourself some downtime?
- Do you have a regular bedtime? Or do you go to bed when there is nothing else to do?
- Do you spend time with your significant other at the end of your day?

Day ends are as important as day starts. Without realising it, you probably have a routine you go through before leaving work and another one you perform as you prepare to go to bed. The question to ask yourself now that you are aware of your routines is: do those routines help or hinder your efforts to be productive both at work and at home?

Now that you've completed a Habits Self-Audit, it's time to consider an action plan to address the issues you identified.

HABITS ACTION PLAN

An action plan is a list of activities designed to take you from where you are to where you want to be. The important part, however, comes after you draw up the plan. Unless you take the actions described in your action plan, it will be nothing more than a well-intentioned list.

DEVELOPING NEW HABITS

If your analysis of the findings of your Habits Self-Audit indicates that you need to develop some new habits or routines, consider using the 42-day project approach to establishing a new routine. This means making a 42-day commitment to establishing any new routine. It will be habitual after that.

STARTING YOUR DAY

Morning routine at home

What changes do you need to make to your domestic morning routine to increase your productivity?

Refer to *Miracle Morning* by Hal Elrod for ideas, if necessary, and write down the morning routine you intend to follow.

Action steps:

Morning routine at work

What changes do you need to make to your start of day routine to increase your productivity?

Refer to *18 Minutes* by Peter Bregman for ideas, if necessary, and write down the morning routine you intend to follow.

Action steps:

DOING THE JOB

If you need some more inspiration before starting on this section of the action plan, I suggest you read *Manage Your Day-To-Day: Build Your Routine, Find Your Focus & Sharpen Your Creative Mind* edited by Jocelyn K Glei.

Structure

Structure your day to enhance your productivity by identifying the best time slots for doing tasks that require high-energy focus, and those you can use for routine administrative tasks. Map out the structure on your calendar and use the appointment feature to block out the times when you do not want to be disturbed. You may need to test this through trial and error to arrive at the most productive structure.

Action steps:

Breaks

Identify the breaks you're planning to take during your day. For example, a five-to-ten-minute break after every hour of work. Make a commitment to yourself to leave the building for lunch. At the very least, stop eating your lunch at your desk. Insert those breaks into your daily structure and start taking them to make them a habit.

Action steps:

Email

Identify the strategies you intend to use to manage your inbox so that you can focus on your work. For example, turn off notifications; action items in your inbox at specific times of the day; pause and review before hitting send. Consider incorporating a specific time or times for dealing with email into your daily structure. Try different strategies to see which one works best for you.

Action steps:

Telephone

Choose a strategy for managing your use of the telephone. For example, letting calls go through to voice mail when you're focusing on a task; planning calls before making them; listening when you're receiving a call.

Note: if you choose to use voice mail to manage your incoming calls, find out how to set your telephone to go straight to voice mail or after a minimum number of rings. There is no point in disturbing everyone around you.

Action steps:

Meetings

Determine how to make the most of any meetings you attend or call. For example, review the list of meetings you attend; plan for meetings beforehand; always circulate an agenda; conduct meetings standing up; don't take your smartphone to meetings. Sometimes, the most productive option is to send someone else.

Action steps:

Collaboration

There is no point in hoarding knowledge or skills others could use, and there is no shame in asking others for assistance - it's one way of acknowledging a co-worker's skill or experience. Sometimes, you'll need to invest a little time showing someone how to do things, but that short-term pain will often provide a long-term gain. Sharing is often the productive option.

Action steps:

Communication

You are often blind to your communication failures and, if you're like most people, you have an incomplete understanding of the art of communication. Start by reading *So What? How to communicate what really matters to your audience* by Mark Magnacca. The secret is it's not about you - it's about what it means to them.

Action steps:

ENDING YOUR DAY
End of day routine at work

What changes do you need to make to your end of day routine to increase your productivity?

Refer to *18 Minutes* by Peter Bregman for ideas, if necessary, and write down the end of day routine you intend to follow.

Action steps:

END OF DAY ROUTINE AT HOME

What changes do you need to make to your domestic end of day routine to increase your productivity?

Refer to *Miracle Morning* by Hal Elrod for ideas, if necessary, and write down the end of day routine you intend to follow.

Action steps:

Measure your progress

There is no point in working on establishing new routines or work habits if they have no impact on your productivity, and you'll soon give up and fall back into your old habits unless you see an improvement in your productivity. This is where you can use those 42-day projects I mentioned.

Set yourself some targets. Consider how you'll work out if you're getting more done or not after you change the way you do things. Remember to notice if you have more energy at the end of the day or whether you feel better about being at work. Find out if you can you stick at something for 42 days.

Action steps:

Now that you've drawn up your Habits Action Plan, make a commitment to act on it. Go to your calendar and set up a monthly review date, just like you would for any other project, and regularly review your progress and update your plan.

Tools

No matter what occupation, profession or craft you're involved in, you depend on tools. They're the things you use to help you perform your job.

When we think of tools, we generally associate them with trades, where you do an apprenticeship to learn how to use your tools of trade. In some professions, like medicine, tools are called instruments but the same mastery learning applies - someone shows you how to use them before they let you loose on the world.

In today's digital world, a lot of us use computers, smartphones and software applications in our work. In some occupations, people are also dealing with an ever-increasing range of sophisticated, automated and expensive machinery.

There is so much technology in workplaces these days that it's easy to lose sight of some of the simpler tools, like a to do list written on a piece of paper or a Post-it note. Yes, even the Post-it note is a tool with many applications, as anyone involved in project management or planning can tell you. Check out their website (www.post-it.com) for inspiration.

The connection between productivity and tools is fairly straight forward. When you know how to use your tools correctly you'll be more productive.

With some tools, all you have to do is read the manual. Others are so sophisticated that you need to take a course and get a certificate.

No matter how you first learn about your tools, the mastery only ever comes from dedicated and intentional practice, and that's different from just using it every day with an indifferent attitude.

Yes, it takes time to master a tool, but that time investment will always be worth it.

The next step is to conduct a self-audit of the tools available to you and to determine if you're making the best use of them. Your findings will help you to develop an action plan for increasing your productivity by mastering your tools.

TOOLS SELF-AUDIT

This is the part where you review your tools to see whether they're facilitating or impeding your productivity.

TOOLS I USE EVERY DAY

List the tools you use to help you perform your job under the following headings using the suggested categories.

For each tool, rate your level of mastery using: E = expert user; A = average user; B = beginner.

Tools I use to do my job

Simple or non-digital tools	Digital tools	Specialised tools or machinery

Tools I use to manage my productivity

Simple or non-digital tools	Digital tools

Tools I use for communication

Simple or non-digital tools	Digital tools

Data analysis

When you start using a new tool, do you use the help function or read the instructions? Or do you ask someone to show you how to use it? Do you take advantage of any training on offer or do you rely on self-instruction?

If you rated yourself as an expert user for a particular tool, do other people ask you how to use that tool?

In my experience, most people settle for being average users and only ever become familiar with a limited range of any tool's features, especially digital tools. If you use a tool daily, I recommend investing the time to master it, and one way of doing that is to teach others how to use it.

ARE YOU USING THE RIGHT TOOLS?

We are creatures of habit and we often stay with the tools we are familiar with, even after we've moved into a new role. Are there any tools you're resisting learning how to use? Are there any that you're resisting letting go?

Take a close look at those tools you use to manage your productivity. How many of them are time management tools? How many are time wasters? Are there any you could stop using?

What about the communication tools you use? Are you using them to hide behind a digital wall instead of talking to people face to face? Do you regard meetings as a communication tool or a waste of time? If you use social media for marketing purposes, how disciplined is your use? Are you online to work or distract yourself from work?

TOOLS I USE OCCASIONALLY

List the tools you use occasionally to help you perform your job using the suggested categories

Simple or non-digital tools	Digital tools	Specialised tools or machinery

Data analysis

In some jobs, there are tools you only use if the need arises. If you work on your own, you have no choice but to learn how to use those tools. If you work with others, sometimes the more productive choice is to allow certain members of your team to become expert users of that tool by directing the work requiring that tool to one or a few team members.

TOOLS I'D LIKE TO HAVE OR LEARN HOW TO USE

List the tools on your wish list using the suggested categories.

Simple or non-digital tools	Digital tools	Specialised tools or machinery

Now that you've completed a Tools Self-Audit, it's time to consider an action plan to address any mastery and productivity issues you have identified.

TOOLS ACTION PLAN

An action plan is a list of activities designed to take you from where you are to where you want to be. The important part, however, comes after you draw up the plan. Unless you take the actions described in your action plan, it will be nothing more than a well-intentioned list.

ACHIEVING MASTERY OF YOUR TOOLS

For every tool that you rated your level of mastery as either average user or beginner, describe what steps you intend to take to increase your level of mastery to expert user. For example, complete any available training courses, read the instruction manual, try out features you don't usually use, or do something yourself that you normally ask someone else to do for you.

Action steps:

PRODUCTIVITY APPS

Before Apple opened its App Store, Microsoft Outlook was probably the most widely used digital productivity management tool. Today, there is an app for just about everything you can think of across all platforms. Make a plan to review your use of productivity apps to ensure you haven't overloaded yourself with digital self-management tasks in the name of productivity.

Action steps:

Communication tools

If you use social media for marketing, write down what you can do to resist the temptation to waste time reading what other people are posting. This may be particularly relevant if you are a self-employed creative.

If you have been hiding behind a wall of digital communication, determine how you can change your communication style to engage with people face to face. Be realistic. You may need to plan a series of small steps to achieve that goal.

Action steps:

Occasional use tools

List the steps you can take to increase the productive use of these tools.

Action steps:

WISH LIST TOOLS

For each tool on your wish list, describe the steps you intend to take to acquire that tool and learn to how to use it.

Action steps:

Now that you've drawn up your Tools Action Plan, make a commitment to act on it. Go to your calendar and set up a monthly review date, just like you would for any other project, and regularly review your progress and update your plan.

Skills

Every job involves a particular set of skills. Some specialised skill sets require years of study; others you can learn on the job. If you have a job or you're in business for yourself, you have a range of skills which will determine how well you perform any given task. You will often get better at some things by simply doing them over and over again. Other tasks will evolve over time and you will need to upgrade your skills to keep up or get ahead.

Soft skills

Some skills required for effective performance are not taught in business schools or training colleges. These are often referred to as soft skills; the skills you use in your day to day interactions with other people. Soft skills can be more important than the highly specialised skills you spend years acquiring and refining. These are the skills of common courtesy, treating people with respect, and knowing how to put patients or clients at ease. Soft skills include knowing the difference between hearing and listening, and between seeing and understanding visual signals when communicating with others. These skills require a level of self-awareness, that is, a willingness to consider how your actions may affect others, and a preparedness to see things from another person's perspective.

Expanding your skill set in a world of change

You're more productive when you work in a position that suits your skill set, however, if you're after a promotion into a position with more responsibility, challenges and money, you need to expand your skill set.

It's tempting to think that knowing how to do your job is enough; it's not. If you want to progress or become a master of any skill you need to continually push yourself to improve and acquire new skills.

When I started work, there were no computers, smartphones and internet. Over the years, I've continually reinvented myself and acquired new skills to remain relevant. You work in a world of continual change. If you're not prepared to embrace change, you will be left behind.

The next step is to conduct a self-audit of your skills and to determine if you're making the best use of them. Your findings will help you to develop an action plan for increasing your productivity by improving your skills.

SKILLS SELF-AUDIT

This is the part where you review your skills to see whether they're facilitating or impeding your productivity.

SKILLS YOU USE TODAY

In the Tools Self-Audit, you looked at the tools you use to do your job and rated your level of mastery of those tools. Your Tools Action Plan is the place for addressing any skills related issues associated with your tools. In this Self-Audit, the focus is on those other skills you need to be productive.

GENERAL SKILLS
Planning

Planning enables you to focus on tasks that are important to you; tasks that are connected to your goals. You can still be busy if you don't plan but you'll be busy doing things related to other people's goals, not your own.

Do you plan what you're going to do each day; each week; each month; each year? Do you set goals?

Time management

We all get the same number of hours each day. The difference between being productive and not is related to what we do with our daily allocation of hours. Time management is actually a misnomer; what we're actually talking about is self-discipline. Planning is one skill. Executing a plan is another skill, and it's in the execution that self-discipline is required.

Do you have the self-discipline to manage the way you use your time?

For an insight into time management, refer to *18 Minutes* by Peter Bregman.

Project management

Project management is applying planning and time management to a specific task or group of tasks called a project, but you don't have to be managing a project to apply project management principles to your work.

Do you use project management principles to manage your workload? If you're not sure what project management principles are, refer to *Everyday Project Management*, book 1 of the Everyday Business Skills series.

Communication

In the workplace, communication is about the deliberate exchange of information to achieve a desired outcome.

- Are you an effective communicator? How do you know?
- Do you confirm that your audience understands your message?
- Do you talk about yourself or do you address the needs of your audience?
- When others communicate with you, do you confirm that you have understood their message or request?

For guidance on evaluating your communication skills, refer to *The Four Conversations: Daily Communication That Gets Results* by Jeffrey and Laurie Ford.

Interpersonal

Most of us work with other people, either as co-workers or customers. Interpersonal skills are those soft skills I mentioned.

- Are you courteous?
- Do you know how to listen?
- Do you treat people with respect?
- Do you know how to empathise and show compassion?

Self-awareness

Being self-aware means having an appreciation of how your behaviour affects others. Is this a new concept for you?

Whether we like it or not, those around us at work judge us by what we do or don't do.

- Do you ever consider how others may perceive you through your actions?
- Do you do what you say you'll do?
- Do you say one thing and do another?
- Do you think about how what you're about to say or do will be perceived by those around you?

Embracing change

There is a spectrum of responses to change that ranges from acceptance through resistance to denial. No matter where you sit on the spectrum, the one undeniable fact of life in the world of work is continual change. Where do you sit on that spectrum? What's your tolerance of change?

Managing others

Managing people is an administrative task that requires its own skill set. If you're in a management position, you need to consider workflow management, allocation of work tasks, performance management, training and coaching, succession planning, leave management, budgeting, corporate targets, meetings, reporting and all those interpersonal skills mentioned above.

- How are you doing? How do you know?
- Are your people driving you nuts?
- What's your management style? Maybe it's you driving your people nuts.
- Have you done any management training? Are you aware there are different management styles?
- Do you have a mentor or someone you can turn to for help when the going gets tough?

Managing up

Sometimes, you find yourself in a position where you're a knowledge expert working for a manager who doesn't have your technical knowledge or experience. Do you know how to manage up or present information so that your manager acts on it? Yes, this is a skill you can develop. It requires self-confidence, an awareness of your manager's communication style, and a commitment to working for the greater good of your firm or organisation.

Coaching

In the work place, a coach is a more like a private tutor than a football coach. Coaching is sharing your experience and skills with someone else to improve their productivity. If you're an expert in your field or you're responsible for the performance of others, do you coach? Have you done any training to become a more effective coach?

Meetings

Meetings are a fact of life in many workplaces. You're either running meetings or attending them.

When you run meetings, do you:

- know why?
- use an agenda?
- have someone record the action items or decisions made?
- know how to get people to participate?
- know how to shut down those individuals that like the sound of their own voice?
- listen or pontificate?

When you attend meetings, do you;

- participate?
- feel comfortable speaking up?
- attend with an open mind or with preconceived ideas?
- prepare before attending?
- take notes?

Leadership

I have purposely separated leadership from management. You don't have to be a manager to be a leader, and many managers are not leaders. Leadership is a state of mind, not a position or a title. Leaders are the people that set standards and inspire others. Leaders are the people that others look to for direction.

Some people appear to be born leaders but that does not stop the rest of us from becoming leaders. Effective leadership, however, requires you to step up to the plate and assume the mantle of leader. It's not something to take on lightly or without preparation.

- Where are you on the leadership spectrum?
- Are you a leader or a follower?
- Do you want to become a leader?
- Are you ready for the responsibility?

For an insight into leadership as a mindset, refer to *Leadership From The Inside Out* by Kevin Cashman.

Data analysis

What do your answers tell you about your current skill set? Is it up-to-date or does it need some enhancing?

SPECIALISED SKILLS

If you're a qualified whatever, just how good a whatever are you? How do you know?

It's easy to get comfortable with your level of skill, but no profession, trade or craft stands still. Even the ways things are done in schools, offices and factories change and evolve. You need to keep up; otherwise you run the risk of becoming a blunt instrument.

- Are you committed to life-long learning?
- Do you participate in continuous professional development or other on-going learning programs?
- If your answer to either of the above is no, why not?

SKILLS REQUIRED FOR THE NEXT STEP ON YOUR CAREER PATH

If you're here working on improving your productive mindset, I guess it's a safe bet you're at least a little ambitious.

Your current skill set may get you noticed. It may even get you promoted, but are you ready for that promotion?

- If you're a generalist with dreams of becoming an expert or a specialist, do you know what skills you need to acquire to transform your dream into your reality? Do you have a plan in place for acquiring those skills?
- If you're dreaming of working your way up the corporate ladder into management, do you know what skills you need to acquire to transform your dream into your reality? Do you have a plan in place for acquiring those skills?
- If your dream is to start your own business, do you know what's involved in setting up a business? Do you have a plan?
- If your dream is to expand your business, do you know what additional skills you'll need to manage that expansion? Do you have a plan?

Now that you've completed a Skills Self-Audit, it's time to consider an action plan to address any mastery and productivity issues you have identified.

Skills Action Plan

An action plan is a list of activities designed to take you from where you are to where you want to be. The important part, however, comes after you draw up the plan. Unless you take the actions described in your action plan, it will be nothing more than a well-intentioned list.

Skills you use today

For each applicable skill, detail the steps you need to take to update or enhance your mastery of that skill. If you need to work on multiple skills, design a schedule that will enable you to spread the task over a period of time. Remember, you still need to do your job while you're enhancing your skill set. Plan to take advantage of any training offered by your employer but be prepared to devote some of your own time to achieving your goals.

If you're self-employed, scheduling skills training into your calendar is one way to remind yourself of your commitment.

General skills

Planning

Action steps:

Time management

Action steps:

Project management

Action steps:

Communication

Action steps:

Interpersonal

Action steps:

Self-awareness

Action steps:

Embracing change

Action steps:

Managing others

Action steps:

Managing up

Action steps:

Coaching

Action steps:

Meetings

Action steps:

Leadership

Action steps:

SPECIALISED SKILLS

Detail your plan for maintaining and updating your specialist skills. For example, enrolling in the continuing professional development training available to you, taking a refresher course or seeking opportunities to practise your skills.

Action steps:

SKILLS REQUIRED FOR THE NEXT STEP ON YOUR CAREER PATH

Detail your plan for finding out what skills you'll need for the next step on your career path, and your plan for acquiring those skills. For example, speak to people doing the thing you aspire to, find a mentor, enrol in a course, ask for stretch assignments.

Action steps:

Now that you've drawn up your Skills Action Plan, make a commitment to act on it. Go to your calendar and set up a monthly review date, just like you would for any other project, and regularly review your progress and update your plan.

Knowledge

Just as any job requires a set of skills, all jobs have a body of knowledge attached to them. For some occupations, that knowledge fits onto a poster stuck on the wall, for many, it would fill a book, while for others, it's held in an ever-increasing library of words. Some of it is not written down. It's in people's heads and is called experience.

Knowledge and skills

A lot of your job-related knowledge is directly associated with the skills required to do your job, and you probably obtained it from training or the on-the-job experience of doing your job. If you work in a profession or trade, you may have spent years studying to acquire that knowledge. And, like skills you use, skill specific knowledge needs to be kept up-to-date.

Knowledge about your job

Not only do you need the knowledge of what is required to do your job, you also need to know about your job. You need to know where your particular job or role fits into the bigger picture of where you work. If you work in a knowledge or awareness bubble, you run the risk of your best efforts being counterproductive for the organisation or business as a whole. For example, if you work in sales and have no awareness of the production process or delivery times, you may get the sale by promising something that can't be done, which generates an unnecessary complaint and gives your firm a poor reputation for service. You think you've done a good job, but your ignorance of where your job fits into the bigger picture has let your firm down. That's not being productive.

You need to be aware of the entire workflow that you are a part of if you want to be productive. By the way, if you are a self-employed sole trader, don't think this doesn't apply to you. You need to know where your business fits into the bigger picture. You need to know what your competitors are doing, what your suppliers can do for you, and what you're capable of delivering.

Experience

When you spend years working for the same firm or in the same line of business, you have the opportunity of acquiring the knowledge of experience, which you can then apply to being more productive. If you're aware of what's going on around you, and if you remember why things were done certain ways in the past, sometimes you can join the dots in a way that people without your experience can't see. For example, because I was aware of a decision made in 2005, about the way procedures would be published to accommodate the structure of a new case management system, when it was decided, in 2015, to modify that case management system, I was able to recognise an opportunity to reduce the number of procedural documents from several hundred to twelve - by applying my knowledge about why something had been done in the past. I also knew who to submit my insight to, and how to package it so that the right decision could be made.

If you're aiming to be productive, it pays to operate beyond the bubble of your day-to-day environment. Network, so that you know who to talk to. Become aware of who holds corporate knowledge about aspects of your work world if you don't have that knowledge yourself, and find out how to present solutions to problems so that decision makers will listen.

The next step is to conduct a self-audit of your knowledge about your job to determine if you're operating in a bubble. Your findings will help you to develop an action plan for increasing your productivity by improving your knowledge about your job.

Knowledge Self-Audit

This is the part where you review your knowledge to see whether it's facilitating or impeding your productivity.

Knowledge and skills

In the Skills Self-Audit, you looked at the skills you use to do your job, and identified any you needed to work on. Your Skills Action Plan is the place to address any knowledge related issues associated with your skills. In this Self-Audit, the focus is on that other knowledge you need to be productive.

Knowledge about your job

To be productive, it's not enough to simply know how to do your job. You need a level of awareness beyond your daily routine. You need to look up from your workstation to see the horizon you're trying to reach, and the team or army of people that you are a part of. If you're in an executive position, you need to take a helicopter view of the landscape of your work environment to avoid becoming distracted by today's urgent issues.

Purpose

Take a moment, and think about what you actually know about your job, apart from what you actually do. For example, what its purpose?

Your job's purpose to your employer may be different to the purpose you have given it. If you want to be a productive contributor to your employer's purpose, it's pretty obvious that you need to align your work activities with your job's purpose. Are they aligned or do you need to make some changes?

The bigger picture

Every job, including yours, has a role in a larger world.

Where does your job fit into the greater scheme of things? What happens to that 'packet' before it arrives on your desk, and what happens to it after you've finished with it?

For example, if you work in a school, do you know what's going on in the classrooms of the year level before the one you teach? And, what about in the year level your students will be moving on to next year? Do you know what's happening in other classes at your year level?

If you work in a large bureaucracy, like a government department or bank for example, do you know what goes on in other parts of the organisation? Are you in contact with people working in other parts of the office? Does the output of your section become the input of another? Do you know how other people do the same job you do?

When you're aware of how your work fits in, and what impact it has on other people working in the same firm or organisation, you can take steps to ensure your work does not cause negative impacts further on down the line. That's being productive, even if it takes you a little more effort to ensure you've corrected your mistakes before passing that 'packet' along.

Data analysis

Be honest, are you working in an awareness bubble, where you know everything about what you do but have no idea where your job fits into the bigger picture?

EXPERIENCE

Your level of experience depends on how long you've been doing something and whether you're open to learning.

Take it from me, it is possible to spend twenty-five years doing the same thing only to have one year's worth of experience - repeated twenty-five times. That's not an approach I recommend, if you're interested in being productive.

When you're committed to productivity, you aim for continual growth at work, and that's how you accumulate experience. That's how you become an expert. To achieve that, you need to be awake when you're at work. You need to notice what happens, and you need to build up a store of knowledge that you can access, whether it's in your head or somewhere on your hard drive.

What is it that you know about your workplace; your business; and your industry because you're involved in it?

What is your work history? What lessons has it taught you?

Are you an expert in a particular aspect of the business?

Data analysis.

Do you hold an accumulation of knowledge gleaned from your time doing whatever it is that you do? What is it? Can you access it? Can you share it?

Now that you've completed a Knowledge Self-Audit, it's time to consider an action plan to address any productivity issues you have identified.

Knowledge Action Plan

An action plan is a list of activities designed to take you from where you are to where you want to be. The important part, however, comes after you draw up the plan. Unless you take the actions described in your action plan, it will be nothing more than a well-intentioned list.

Knowledge about your job
Purpose

List the actions you plan to take to align your everyday activities with your job's purpose.

For example, read your firm's mission or vision statement and its strategic plan, and talk about how your role fits in with your manager, team or co-workers.

Action steps:

The bigger picture

List the actions you plan to take to increase the size of your awareness bubble, so that you'll have a better understanding of where your job fits into the bigger picture of your workplace.

For example, if you're operating inside a small awareness bubble focused on your job, determine who you need to talk to, what existing information you need to read, and what questions you could ask to increase your level of understanding of where your job fits into the bigger picture.

Action steps:

EXPERIENCE

List the actions you plan to take to access your experience based knowledge and share it.

For example, write out your work history and highlight the lessons you have learnt, and record what you know about your workplace; your business; and your industry.

Action steps:

Now that you've drawn up your Knowledge Action Plan, make a commitment to act on it. Go to your calendar and set up a monthly review date, just like you would for any other project, and regularly review your progress and update your plan.

Community

No-one, not even those of you that are self-employed sole traders, works in isolation. We are all surrounded by a community of people: employers, managers, co-workers, customers, suppliers, competitors, family and friends.

Within that community you can find mentors; people who will sell you training courses online; authors that have written books you can read; and people to talk things over with. Communities are where we find our friends, have fun, and support each other.

It may be helpful to think of your work and social communities as separate groups. For some, there is a significant overlap between those groups but, for many of us, the people we live with are not the people we work with.

We considered the people you live with when we discussed your lifestyle. Here, our focus is on the people you work with.

Work community

Your work community is a group that you can tap into and contribute to. Not only can you receive assistance and guidance from its members, you can also give those things to others in the community. The value of your work community to you will be determined by who's in it, and your level of participation in its activities.

Depending on what sort of business you work in, your work community may encompass people outside of your immediate workplace. For example, the members of any professional associations you choose to join or your network of contacts within your industry.

Work communities usually also contain a few negative members. So, just like you choose your friends, it also pays to choose who you share your plans with at work, as well. Not everybody is helpful. Not everybody is interested in being more productive. In fact, some people will be threatened by any change in your behaviour and may actively discourage you. But, don't let them discourage you. One of the secrets to being productive is to surround yourself with people who think about work the same way you do.

The next step is to conduct a self-audit of your community to determine if you're associating with the right people. Your findings will help you to develop an action plan for increasing your productivity by associating with people who think about work the same way you do.

COMMUNITY SELF-AUDIT

This is the part where you review your community to see whether it's facilitating or impeding your productivity.

SOCIAL COMMUNITY

In the Lifestyle Self-Audit, you looked at the community you share your life with, and identified any issues you needed to work on. Your Lifestyle Action Plan is the place to address any community issues associated with your lifestyle. In this Self-Audit, the focus is on your work community.

WORK COMMUNITY

- Who do you know at work? Make a list.
- Do you know people outside your immediate work team? Who are they? What do they do? What can they teach you? What can you teach them?
- Do you attend work related social functions?
- Who do you discuss your dreams and plans with at work?
- Do you have a mentor? Do you mentor others?
- If you have a problem at work, who do you discuss it with?
- Are you a member of any professional or trade associations? Do you attend meetings, training sessions or functions?
- How do you get on with the people you spend most of your working day with?
- Who are the centres of negative influence in your workplace? Do you spend any time with them?

Data analysis

Take a look at who you're spending your time with at work. Are you participating within the wider work community or restricting yourself to a few people in your immediate area?

Who could you include within your work community? Who should you avoid?

FOR MANAGERS.

Often, your productivity is measured by the output of the team or teams you manage. You have an opportunity, perhaps an obligation, to help your team members develop a productive mindset. Sometimes, that's a real challenge but your team is part of your work community. What can you do to help them develop a productive mindset?

Now that you've completed a Community Self-Audit, it's time to consider an action plan to increase the size and quality of your work community.

COMMUNITY ACTION PLAN

An action plan is a list of activities designed to take you from where you are to where you want to be. The important part, however, comes after you draw up the plan. Unless you take the actions described in your action plan, it will be nothing more than a well-intentioned list.

WORK COMMUNITY

List the steps you intend taking to increase the size and quality of your work community.

For example, network within your firm; network within your industry; join a professional or trade association; attend meetings of associations you belong to; seek a mentor; offer to mentor younger workers; stop spending time with people who only see the negative side of things or always bad mouth the firm.

Action steps:

FOR MANAGERS

List the steps you intend taking to help your team develop a more productive mindset.

For example, identify any training or coaching you can offer; share some or all of the exercise in this book with them; talk to them about how their jobs fit into the bigger picture.

Action steps:

Now that you've drawn up your Community Action Plan, make a commitment to act on it. Go to your calendar and set up a monthly review date, just like you would for any other project, and regularly review your progress and update your plan.

Summary

You've studied the text, done the analysis and written your action plans. Now it's time to put those plans into action.

Most personal growth and expansion is incremental, so don't attempt to address everything at once. Pick one area to work with and start with that. My suggestion is that you start with your Lifestyle Action Plan. When you've worked on that area, start on another.

To be honest, you're never going to finish working on yourself and, from my perspective, that's a good thing. The world doesn't stand still while you're growing, after all. So, as soon as you reach one level, plan to review your progress, and then push on to the next within your changed circumstances.

If you get the opportunity to participate in a training course that furthers your skills and knowledge, take it. I learnt a lot from courses offered by my employers over the years and, now that I'm self-employed, I'm still taking courses to increase my knowledge and skills.

Committing to lifelong learning is something that will help you continue to grow and expand, learn new skills and explore different perspectives. I recommend it.

On the next page, you'll find a list of the books I referred you to throughout the text. Some of my favourite business books are in that list. I encourage you to read them.

Take time to celebrate the achievement of your milestones. Rewarding yourself for making plans and following through with the actions you planned will help you stay committed.

Finally, I encourage you to share your knowledge and insights with anyone inspired by your reinvigorated productive mindset.

Further reading

Calling in the One by Katherine Woodward Thomas.

Change Your Thoughts, Change Your Life by Wayne Dyer.

18 Minutes by Peter Bregman.

Everyday Project Management by Peter Mulraney,

How to Live a Good Life by Jonathan Fields.

Leadership From The Inside Out by Kevin Cashman.

Liminal Thinking by Dave Gray.

Manage Your Day-To-Day: Build Your Routine, Find Your Focus & Sharpen Your Creative Mind edited by Jocelyn K Glei.

So What? How to Communicate What Really Matters to Your Audience by Mark Magnacca.

The Four Conversations: Daily Communication That Gets Results by Jeffrey and Laurie Ford.

The Pause Principle by Kevin Cashman.

Think or Swim: The One Choice That Changes Everything by Gina Millicone-Long.

A Note from Peter

Everyday Productivity is the second book in the Everyday Business Skills series, in which I share the knowledge I gained from a forty-year career in education, banking, and government.

If you found it useful, please consider writing a review or sharing the book's details on social media to help other readers find the book.

In addition to the Everyday Business Skills series, I have several other books you might enjoy reading.

You can find details about all of my books and read my blog on www.petermulraney.com, where you can join my Crime Readers Group and download a free copy of my novella: *Deadly Sands* or subscribe to my monthly newsletter 'Insights from a crime writing mystic' and download a free copy of *A Question of Perspective*.

Thank you for buying the book.

Peter Mulraney

Also by Peter Mulraney

Everyday Business Skills

Everyday Project Management

Everyday Money Management

Living Alone Series

After She's Gone

Cooking 4 One

Sanity Savers

Living Alone (Collection)

Inspector West Series

After

The Holiday

Holy Death

Whistleblower

Twisted Justice

The East Park Syndicate

Novella

The New Girlfriend

Stella Bruno Investigates

The Identity Thief

A Gun of Many Parts

Bones in the Forest

A Deadly Game of Hangman

Taken

Fallout

The Identity Thief Collection

The Fallout Collection

Writings of the Mystic

Sharing the Journey: Reflections of a Reluctant Mystic

A Question of Perspective

My Life is My Responsibility: Insights for Conscious Living

I Am Affirmations: The Power of Words

Beyond the Words: Reflections on I Am Affirmations

Mystical Journey: A Handbook for Modern Mystics

Sharing the Journey Coloring Books

Mandalas

Mandalas by 3

Sharing the Journey Coloring Journals

Sharing the Journey

Discovery

Reflection

www.ingramcontent.com/pod-product-compliance
Lightning Source LLC
Chambersburg PA
CBHW082243300426
44110CB00036B/2433